Robert Quackenbush
Who Said There's No Man on the Moon?
A Story of Jules Verne

Prentice-Hall, Inc.
ENGLEWOOD CLIFFS, NEW JERSEY

Printed in the United States of America   •J

Prentice-Hall International, Inc., London
Prentice-Hall of Australia, Pty. Ltd., Sydney
Prentice-Hall Canada, Inc., Toronto
Prentice-Hall Hispanoamericana, S.A., Mexico
Prentice-Hall of India Private Ltd., New Delhi
Prentice-Hall of Japan, Inc., Tokyo
Prentice-Hall of Southeast Asia Pte. Ltd., Singapore
Whitehall Books Limited, Wellington, New Zealand
Editora Prentice-Hall do Brasil LTDA., Rio. de Janeiro

10   9   8   7   6   5   4   3   2   1

Library of Congress Cataloging in Publication Data

Quackenbush, Robert M.
   Who said there's no man on the moon?

   Summary: A biography of the nineteenth-century
author whose novels of science fiction adventure
predicted space travel, the submarine, and other
modern achievements.
   1. Verne, Jules, 1828-1905—Juvenile literature.
2. Authors, French—19th century—Biography—Juvenile
literature. 3 Science fiction, French—History and
criticism—Juvenile literature. [1. Verne, Jules,
1828-1905. 2. Authors, French. 3. Science fiction—
History and criticism] I. Title.
PQ2469.Z5Q33   1988   843′.8[B]   [92]   84-22314
ISBN 0-13-958430-7

Jules Verne was born in the seaport town of Nantes, France on February 8, 1828. He was the oldest of five children. He had a brother, Paul, who was a year younger, and three sisters. Paul and Jules were close all their lives. Their father was a lawyer and their mother came from a family of shipbuilders and sea captains. As a boy, Jules dreamed of traveling to exotic lands. When he was twelve, he tried to run away to sea on a ship that was sailing to India. His father pursued him in a steamboat and took him off the ship. From then on Jules made up his mind to travel only in his imagination and to become a writer someday.

9

Jules found that it wasn't so easy to become a writer. Though he was educated to be a lawyer at his father's insistence, he refused to work at anything but writing. Living in Paris in the 1850's, he managed to get a few articles published in magazines and a short play produced on the stage. It was not enough to earn a living. Often he had only enough money for a meal of dried prunes. So he was forced to look for other work. For a while he was a law clerk. After that he became a theater secretary and supervised the production of shows. Then he met and fell in love with Honorine Morel, a young widow with two children. He became a stockbroker so he could get married and support his family. However, he didn't earn much as a stockbroker and they had to live in a tiny apartment. Even so, Honorine supported her husband's desire to become a writer. She encouraged him to create stories and plays in his free time. But by the time his only son Michel was born, in 1861, Verne, now thirty-three, still had little success as a writer.

11

Two years later, Honorine rescued from the burning stove a manuscript that Verne had tossed there when he was unable to get it published. And it was a good thing she did because soon afterwards Verne heard about a publisher, Peter Hetzel, who might be interested in it. It was a nonfiction scientific account of what it would be like to explore unknown Africa in a balloon. At the time, the idea of balloon transportation was very new and undeveloped. Hetzel read the manuscript and suggested that Verne rewrite it as a fictional adventure story based on scientific fact. Verne rushed home and rewrote it and took it back to Hetzel. The new version was an exciting tale about an explorer named Fergusson, a big-game hunter named Kennedy, and a servant named Joe, who fly across Africa from east to west in a balloon in search of the source of the Nile River. It told how the three characters survive all sorts of adventures and narrow escapes on their journey. After reading *Five Weeks in a Balloon*, Hetzel was so thrilled that he immediately gave Verne a twenty-year contract to write two books a year.

Five Weeks in a Balloon was a huge success. It brought Verne worldwide fame as a writer. Now he could stop trying to be a businessman. He could devote his full time to writing about his imaginary travels. His next book, called *The Adventures of Captain Hatteras*, took his readers on a perilous trek to explore the unknown lands of the Arctic. Following this, he took them on still another exciting adventure to view underground seas and pre-historic creatures in *Journey to the Center of the Earth*. Both books reflected the latest scientific knowledge and theories of the time about the earth's evolution. They were met with the same excitement as the first book and Verne's success was assured. The Vernes moved to a larger home and bought new furniture. But with his success came an endless stream of social affairs and parties. Soon Verne grew restless. He longed for quiet to write his books. He moved his family to a quiet seashore town, the tiny fishing village of Le Crotoy. As if that wasn't enough, he bought a yacht and proceeded to do his writing on the water where no one could disturb him.

Every year revealed new voyages by the founder of a new kind of literature, modern science fiction. Before Verne began a book, he read hundreds of others to make sure he understood the subject thoroughly. This was how he went about writing his next "extraordinary voyage." It was called *From the Earth to the Moon*. In this amazing work, Verne launched the first space capsule ever described in fiction. He used current theories about motion, gravity, space, and the moon to tell how a gun club from Maryland launched the capsule in Florida. The public adored the fanciful idea because Verne had taken the myth of a moon voyage into the realm of reality. But what is surprising to us today is that Verne predicted an event one hundred years into the future. And just as it was in his book, our first real rocket to the moon was launched in Florida. He developed a sixth sense of just how the future marvels of science would come to pass. Like his space capsule, many of his imagined inventions served as blueprints for future inventors.

17

Readers were left hanging in suspense at the end of *From the Earth to the Moon*. They wondered if Verne's astronauts got to their destination. More than that, they wanted to know if the legend about the man on the moon—that life existed there—was true. And they were depending on Verne to tell them. But in spite of all his research, Verne could not answer that question. In his sequel called *Around the Moon* he avoided the question with a surprising twist. Just as his astronauts are about to land on the moon, their projectiles take them instead back to earth. So Verne didn't have to answer the question because his astronauts didn't land on the moon. Nevertheless he took his astronauts on a thrilling journey, landed them in the Pacific, and had them welcomed home with a national celebration, just as it was to happen in reality in the 1960's.

18

In 1867, Verne decided to take his first real, honest-to-goodness voyage. He went to England and boarded the *Great Eastern*, the biggest and most impressive steamship in existence. The voyage would take two weeks from England to America. Then there would be a stay of one week in America before embarking on another long sail back to France. Verne traveled with his brother, who had done what Verne wanted to do as a child—Paul had become an experienced seaman in order to see the world. Verne liked the trip from England and kept a journal each day. When the ship docked in New York, Verne and Paul had just enough time to see a Broadway show and to travel to Buffalo for a quick look at Niagara Falls, before returning to the ship for the long voyage home. But on the way back, Verne felt bored and restless. He didn't like the idea of repeating the same experience at sea. Afterwards he had no more interest in long journeys except in his imagination. But later he did write about his *Great Eastern* adventure in a book called *The Floating City*.

Upon his return from America, Verne was inspired to work on one of the greatest adventure stories ever written, *20,000 Leagues Under the Sea*. The new book was about a submarine, decades before such a craft was successfully built. Verne's fictional submarine is commanded by the mysterious Captain Nemo, whose name means "No One." It is propelled by electricity and the way it works is quite similar to modern undersea craft. Verne named it the *Nautilus* after Robert Fulton's submarine that had been tried without success many years earlier in France. When the book was published in 1870, Verne was presented with the Legion of Honor for his "extraordinary voyages." It is a medal given to important military men and civilians who have brought honor to France.

22

Verne's delight about his recent honor and the publication of his new books was quickly dampened. In July of that same year, 1870, war broke out between France and Prussia. Verne was given orders to be on the lookout for enemy ships from his yacht. He sent Honorine and the children to her family in Amiens for safety and proceeded to follow orders. But the enemy had nothing to fear; the *St. Michel II* (Verne's second yacht) carried twelve seedy army veterans and a small cannon that was about as effective as a popgun. After only eight months, the French lost the war. France had to give up two frontier provinces and was plunged into national debt. Verne decided to write something lighthearted to cheer his sad nation. He invented a character named Phileas Fogg who bets that he can journey around the world in the then unheard-of time of eighty days. As Fogg starts out on his impossible journey, adventure piles on adventure. At one point Fogg finds his lost valet, Passepartout, working in a restaurant in China by supporting a team of clowns on his shoulders. The book ends with Fogg arriving ten minutes ahead of schedule and winning the bet. *Around the World in Eighty Days* was a smash. It was produced as a play and made a fortune.

Verne became giddy with riches. His giddiness inspired a new book, *Dr. Ox*. This story tells about a visit to a make-believe town in Flanders that functions in slow motion. It is a place where everyone eats slowly, talks slowly, dances slowly, and where no one, not even the dogs and cats, has a fight because it would take too much energy. Along comes Dr. Ox to introduce gas street lamps to the town. Soon after his arrival, fruits, vegetables and flowers grow to an enormous size. Dogs now chase cats. A whole opera is performed in a few minutes. People dance, really dance, as though their feet were being driven by electric shocks. Then Dr. Ox's gasworks blows up and everything returns to the way it was. In the end, it is discovered that Dr. Ox had been pumping pure oxygen into the air through his street lamps in an experiment to liven up the town. Actually, this could not happen, but Verne based his idea on what was known about oxygen at the time. *Dr. Ox* remains one of Verne's funniest stories and contains the shortest chapter ever written, forty-one words!

In the next few years, Verne was to become truly famous, a household name. He was as well known as our movie stars are today. Much of this had to do with *Around the World in Eighty Days*, Verne's most successful novel. But his masterpiece was *The Mysterious Island*, which was published in 1875, after many years of preparation. It tells the story of five men who escape their captors in a balloon during America's Civil War. Their balloon is driven off course and they land on an unknown island in the Pacific. How they survive on an island without provisions is the focus of this thrilling adventure. With the scientific mind of Jules Verne helping the colonists, they climb the ladder of civilization year by year. They learn how to build fires with the crystals from two watches, to make knives from the collar of a dog, to make iron, and finally to make their own dynamite to blast a home for themselves out of solid rock to protect them from hurricanes. And, as with most of Verne's stories, there is a surprising twist at the end. It involves the reappearance of Captain Nemo and the discovery of his true identity.

In 1876 Verne looked to Russia for an imaginary journey. For three days he read everything he could find in libraries about Siberia. When he was satisfied that he could picture in his mind exactly what it was like, he attached a story to the information he had gained. He titled the book *Michael Strogoff*. It tells the story of a loyal messenger who races across Siberia to warn the Czar's brother of a traitor. This was one of the few times Verne did not use science and machinery to tell a story. But he succeeded in writing an adventure that was one of the most popular of his "extraordinary voyages." He wrote it with a surprise ending and with an eye to the stage. Humor and drama abound in it, such as when Michael ducks across a battlefield into a hut. There he finds a telegraph clerk who is unaware of the battle going on outside even though bullets whiz right by his window. The book was an immediate success. Just as Verne hoped, it was produced as a play and brought him even more wealth.

After the success of *Michael Strogoff*, Verne bought his third yacht and named it *St. Michel III*. With its crew of nine he would spend more than half the year at sea writing his imaginary adventures. But he did not sail far, mind you. Wherever he sailed, great crowds waited at the docks to greet him and there were fireworks displays in his honor. All this attention and the close relationship Verne had with his brother made Paul's son Gaston envious. In 1886, suffering from a mental breakdown, Gaston shot Verne in the leg and made him lame. After that, Verne decided to stay out of the limelight as much as possible. He sold his yacht and wrote only in his study at Amiens in the house where the family had been living since 1871. There he finished *Clipper of the Clouds*, with its Nemo-like character named Robur. In this story Robur's combination helicopter and flying machine, the *Albatross*, rescues the balloon, the *Go Ahead*. The book became a huge success. People were becoming more air-minded every day. They had learned to pay attention to Verne's predictions. There was no question after reading the book that heavier-than-air craft would take to the sky in the near future.

"YOU HAVE TRAVELED A GREAT DEAL, OF COURSE, MONSIEUR VERNE."
"MAIS NON, JUST A TOURIST IN THE CHANNEL AND IN THE MEDITERRANEAN."
"IS THAT ALL? SO YOU NEVER MET ANY CANNIBALS?"
"I KNEW BETTER THAN THAT."
"NOR ANY CHINESE?"
"NEVER."
"AND YOU DIDN'T CIRCUMNAVIGATE THE GLOBE?"
"NOT EVEN THAT." —1898 INTERVIEW—

By the turn of the century, Verne's predictions were catching up with him. A successful submarine had been built. Electricity was already lighting the world. Automobiles were appearing on the roads. Industry was moving at a fast pace with its giant machines. Now, Verne was concerned that the Machine Age would get out of control and lead to dictatorships. He expressed this concern in *Master of the World*, written in 1902, which marked the return of Robur as a dangerous madman. Robur owns a supercar, the *Terror*, which can be instantly adapted into an automobile, a boat, a submarine, or an airplane. With his machine, Robur intends to rule the world. In the end, his madness destroys him and the hero, Inspector Strock, survives to let the world know it is safe once more. This was typical of the books Verne wrote during his last years. He hoped that they would serve as a warning to readers that science and technology should be used to build a better world. This can happen only if nations learn to cooperate and use their powers wisely.

Epilogue

Because Jules Verne did not want to tell the world much about himself, very few actual facts are known about his life. But, as artists and writers do, he revealed himself in his books which brought him love and admiration from many people. When he died on March 24, 1905, at the age of seventy-seven, five thousand people came to his funeral. Though he is often called the inventor of science fiction, this is not accurate. Science fiction dates back to ancient times and to the works of Homer and the Arabian tales of Sinbad the Sailor. But Verne combined scientific fact with his fiction to give it a feeling of reality. That is why he is often called the father of modern science fiction and the greatest storyteller of them all. Next to Lenin and Shakespeare, he is the most translated author today. His books have been published in 104 languages. For a boy who never made his runaway trip to India, he more than made up for it in his imagination and by sharing his "extraordinary voyages" with us in the sixty-odd books he wrote. His works made many young readers see visions, made them wish they could do great things, and inspired them to make their wishes come true. They grew up to attain great scientific achievements and include:

Robert H. Goddard, rocket expert
Wernher von Braun, rocket expert
Norbert Casteret, explorer of caves and caverns
Simon Lake, designer of submarines
Guglielmo Marconi, inventor of the wireless telegraph